Book Description

You want the top spot on Google, but do you know how to get there?

Google Search is extremely competitive, and SEO is what drives results. The rewards are huge, but it's confusing to implement.

You're not alone if you're seeking SEO advice. Most website owners go about doing the wrong things and leave themselves vulnerable to Google's latest updates.

This stops now. *The One-Month Blueprint to #1* is going to give you a structured list of items that you can easily implement today on your website. No fancy technical stuff here, just advice that works.

Yoav Tchelet has helped some of the largest companies in the world (Kellogg's, FIFA, and Nestlé, to name a few) master their web presence, and in this book he's going to teach you:

- How to find what Google really wants. Hint: They give it to you for free!
- The easy and simple way of carrying out keyword research
- The nine SEO factors that you need to optimise today
- How the latest developments are changing the game . . . and how you can use this to your advantage

. . . and so much more!

Stop trying to implement tired old SEO advice and learn to do things the right way instead. The big boys do this already and now so can you!

The One-Month Blueprint to #1

The SEO Playbook That Will Get Your Business to #1 on Search Engines

Yoav Tchelet

© **Copyright 2020 - All rights reserved.**

The content contained within this book may not be reproduced, duplicated or transmitted without direct written permission from the author or the publisher.

Under no circumstances will any blame or legal responsibility be held against the publisher, or author, for any damages, reparation, or monetary loss due to the information contained within this book, either directly or indirectly.

Paperback ISBN: 9798573890234

Book Cover Design ebooklaunch.com

Legal Notice:

This book is copyright protected. It is only for personal use. You cannot amend, distribute, sell, use, quote or paraphrase any part, or the content within this book, without the consent of the author or publisher.

Disclaimer Notice:

Please note the information contained within this document is for educational and entertainment purposes only. All effort has been executed to present accurate, up to date, reliable, complete information. No warranties of any kind are declared or implied. Readers acknowledge that the author is not engaged in the rendering of legal, financial, medical or professional advice. The content within this book has been derived from various sources. Please consult a licensed professional before attempting any techniques outlined in this book.

By reading this document, the reader agrees that under no circumstances is the author responsible for any losses, direct or indirect, that are incurred as a result of the use of the information contained within this document, including, but not limited to, errors, omissions, or inaccuracies.

Table of Contents

Introduction
    Paid Versus Organic
        About Me
Chapter 1: How Does Google Work?
    Dissecting Relevance
        Backlinks
        Page Speed
        UX
        Content Quality
        Site Authority
        Security
        Mobile Friendliness
        Structured Data
        Voice Search Optimised
Chapter 2: Factor #1 – Search Intent
    Keyword Research
        How to Conduct Keyword Research
        Competition
Chapter 3: SEO Factor #2 – Backlinks
    Relevance
    Promotion
        Active Outreach
        Guest Post
        Podcasts
        Broken-Link Building
        Resource Pages
Chapter 4: SEO Factor #3 – Page Speed
    Compress Images
    Browser Caching
    Minify HTML
    Remove Excess Plugins and Scripts
    Use a CDN
Chapter 5: SEO Factor #4 – User Experience

- Metrics
  - CTR
  - Dwell Time
    - Quick and Snappy Intros
    - Long-Form Content
    - Easy to Read
    - Videos and Alternate Content
    - Internal Links
- Chapter 6: SEO Factor #5 – Content Quality
  - Freshness
  - Accuracy
  - Depth
- Chapter 7: SEO Factor #6 – Site Authority
  - YMYL
    - Keys to Authority
- Chapter 8: SEO Factor #7 – Security and Mobile Friendliness
  - Security
  - Mobile Friendliness
- Chapter 9: SEO Factor #8 – Structured Data
  - Understanding Structured Data
- Chapter 10: SEO Factor #9 – Voice Search Optimization
  - Create FAQ Pages
  - Capture the Snippet
    - Clean HTML
    - Formatted H2 and H3 Headers
    - Crafted Content
  - Write Naturally
    - Keep it Simple
    - Boost Speed
- Conclusion
- References
  - Image References

Introduction

Traffic. It's the lifeblood of every online enterprise. There are endless reams of literature written about how to drive traffic to your website and business. Secret sauces and hidden keys are promised. The truth is that driving traffic to your website is extremely simple. Yet, this doesn't mean it's easy. Like everything else, the simplest things are hard to execute.

One reason for this is the changing nature of the web. You might not realise this, but the internet that existed between 2010 and 2015 no longer exists. Back then, you could reasonably expect your content to be shared across social media widely by simply posting it on a platform. For example, the reach that a single Facebook post had in this period was exponential.

Not only was it shared amongst those on your friends list, but your content had a good chance of showing up on the feeds of people who weren't connected to you in any way. Many businesses took advantage of this and set up Facebook pages and groups to drive traffic to their websites.

Large corporations such as Buzzfeed took advantage of the virality that social media could generate, created tons of listicles ('25 Ways to Look Cool' and so on), and turned themselves into media houses overnight. This virality, referred to as organic reach, was high on all platforms.

YouTube functioned the same way, and a single video could reach an audience of potentially millions in no time. Pinterest gained popularity as a visual search engine, and for a long time, bloggers used it as a way to drive traffic to their websites. Instagram worked the same way, with a single post showing up in the feeds of millions of people and popular posts remaining at the top of users' recommendations for a long time.

Posting on social media became a go-to strategy for all businesses. Web traffic experts began recommending that businesses and websites post content on social media by default. If you weren't on all platforms at once, you clearly weren't serious about success.

Then one fine day, all of this changed. Everyone had fallen into a neatly laid trap that was set up by the social media companies.

Paid Versus Organic

Examining this state of affairs from the social media company's point of view is instructive. These companies don't create anything. They rely on their users to generate content. People will create content only if they're guaranteed exposure. After all, what's the point of creating awesome content if no one gets to see it?

The problem for the social media company is that allowing people to share content widely (high organic reach) is not a good business model. How can the company monetise such content? They can force ads into the content, but this ruins the browsing experience. Facebook was one of the first companies to understand this.

Obviously, there's no way to figure out if they realised this or whether they strategised this ahead of time. It doesn't matter. The fact is that these companies lured people in and got them accustomed to creating content. Imagine a business that generated millions of dollars by posting on Facebook. These businesses began relying on social media to generate traffic.

Facebook recognised this and changed their algorithm. They drastically reduced their organic reach and rendered Facebook pages close to useless because of it. You might think this would have angered businesses and would have resulted in them moving away from the platform. However, they couldn't.

For starters, no other platform gave them similar exposure. Secondly, inertia and the high cost of switching meant they were forced to play by the new rules. These were to pay for exposure or receive none. The average Facebook post these days is only shared between people who are likely to comment on it with some regularity. A large 'Friends' list means nothing. In effect, your post is going to be viewed by around 16% of your connections (Bernazzani, 2014).

Paid marketing became the norm, and all of a sudden free traffic flow was choked. While all of this was going on, Google kept tweaking their algorithm. There were major changes, but unlike social media companies, Google did not force its users to pay for traffic. After all, the company could hardly shut down internet search results.

The result of all these developments is that search engine optimisation (SEO) remains the only way to guarantee organic reach. SEO has changed over the years, since Google is notoriously secretive about what works. This is understandable. It cuts right to the heart of what Google's algorithm and business model is about. It also prevents people from gaming the system and demoting genuinely helpful content.

Investing in SEO remains one of the best decisions a business can make. This is because SEO rewards you for providing value. You don't need to pay for exposure and neither do you need to worry about algorithm changes wrecking your business model. As long as you provide good content and follow the right practices, you will be rewarded.

Doing this in practice is difficult, though. What exactly constitutes as being 'helpful' content? Some people think it has to do with the length of your posts, others think it's all about backlinks, some think backlinks are overrated, and so on. There's a lot of conflicting advice about how to generate organic traffic.

This is what I'm going to teach you in this book.

About Me

As a digital and information technology executive with over twenty years of cross-industry expertise, I've seen many changes occur. I was around when the internet was still in its Web 1.0 incarnation and have seen radical shifts in the way it has been used. I've founded a number of startups, including Askvised, which is a global digital and business transformation consultancy.

In short, I drive change and innovation when it comes to digital marketing and help businesses transform their goals. I've worked with some of the world's leading brands such as FIFA, Nestlé, and Kellogg's. Combining strategic and operational experience, I bring businesses a wealth of knowledge that they can use to achieve their goals.

I will help you stand out in Google's eyes. That's what this book is all about. Are you ready to rise to #1 in search results and receive millions of eyeballs on your content? If so, let's move forward and see how it's done!

Chapter 1: How Does Google Work?

Many people have tried to reverse engineer how Google's algorithm works. This is a close-to-hopeless task to attempt because their algorithm keeps evolving and gets smarter by the day. Google employs advanced machine learning and artificial intelligence (AI) to drive search-related results. It's a bit like trying to predict exactly how a wave in the ocean is going to crash onto the shore.

This doesn't mean you shouldn't care about Google's work methods. It's just that you need to take a big-picture view. Google is more than happy to tell you what they're looking for, as long as you ask the right questions. The biggest hint as to what they're looking for is present right in their mission statement.

I'm not kidding, they really do tell you exactly what they want to do. Here's an excerpt from their statement (*How Google Search Works | Our Mission*, 2019, Maximize Access to Information Section, para. 1):

> Our company mission is to organize the world's information and make it universally accessible and useful . . . . We use approachable language and design to guide you through your experience on Search, and test our approach broadly to make sure we're presenting information in the most useful way . . . . We don't charge anyone to appear in our search index. Whether a business, individual or organization buys ads is not a factor in our search algorithms. We never provide special treatment to advertisers in how our search algorithms rank their websites, and nobody can pay us to do so.

In short, they want to organise the world's information, present it in an easily understood manner, and do not charge you for access. Pretty simple to understand, isn't it? These brief statements drive every decision Google has taken since inception. Instead of trying to figure out the technicalities of SEO and the algorithm, if more businesses paid attention to this, they'd be much more successful.

Organising the world's information means they need to present the most relevant and informative results for a search topic. If you search for dog food and receive results about fish tanks, this is neither an organised result nor is it helpful. If you search for dog food and receive results related to dog food but cannot understand what's written on those pages, this isn't relevant or helpful either.

Information also has a habit of becoming outdated. This means Google needs to constantly remain alert and figure out whether the information they're presenting is relevant or not. In short, relevance is at the core of Google's search algorithm. Understanding what constitutes relevance will ensure you figure out what SEO is all about.

Dissecting Relevance

From publicly available information, we can safely say that Google's algorithm takes over two hundred factors into account when it comes to figuring out the relevance of content. This seems like a gargantuan list but by using some common sense, and by looking at the bigger picture, we can figure out some of the most important things that Google looks at.

First off, let's begin by understanding what relevance even means. The dictionary definition of relevance is 'the quality or state of being closely connected or appropriate' (thank you, Google)! If your content is closely connected to what a user is searching for and is appropriate to their search intent, your content is relevant.

Search intent is the key in all of this. For example, if someone searches for 'best dog food,' what is their intent? There could be many things that this search term implies. The user could be searching for:

1. The best dog food brands
2. The healthiest dog food
3. Dog food that provides the best value for money
4. Is organic dog food the best dog food?
5. Does good dog food contain chemical additives?
6. What sort of effects does the best dog food produce in their dog?

. . . and so on. People often say (type) one thing while they mean something else. Google would have a pretty simple job if everybody in the world adhered to a common language that operated on the basis of very specific parameters. However, that's not how people work. Who would want to live in such a world anyway?

In order to provide relevant content, Google needs to understand and guess the user's search intent. For this reason, you will find that many search phrases will contain results that address various intents. The only exception is if the search term is very specific so as to communicate intent clearly. For example, 'best Indian restaurant near me' is a very specific search term, and its intent is clear.

Displaying a list of Greek restaurants 100 miles away from the person is clearly irrelevant. Your content needs to take search intent into account as well, and you'll learn all about this shortly. For now, let's take a brief look at some of the other factors that drive relevance.

Backlinks

Let's imagine a scenario where you're trying to figure out what you want to eat. You want to reward yourself with a great meal and feel like having some Indian food. Now imagine the internet didn't exist. What do you do? The thing that people used to do was to call their friends and ask if they knew of a great Indian restaurant. Word of mouth was what drove traffic to these places.

Google has brought that principle to search. The online equivalent of word-of-mouth recommendations are backlinks. If someone says your content is great, Google trusts you more.

Page Speed

The only thing worse than no internet is slow internet. We have zero patience for pages that take forever to load. Google understands this. If a page loads slowly, the user will find it irrelevant, no matter how great the information is, and will navigate away from it. Promoting slow-to-load pages in search results will lead to people distrusting Google's recommendations. Page speed matters a lot.

UX

UX stands for user experience. It covers many things that you'll learn about shortly. How well is the information organised on the page? How well is it structured? Is the information clear and easy to understand? All of this ties into how relevant the user thinks a search result is.

Content Quality

This is pretty simple to understand. How good is your content? Is it useful for your users, or is it a mishmash of irrelevant stuff? This ties directly to the relevance factor of your content and should be pretty easy to understand. We'll explore this in greater depth later in this book.

Site Authority

How authoritative is your website? Think of it this way: If you're seeking medical advice, would you listen to a doctor or to your friendly neighbourhood quack? Who is more authoritative on the subject? Authority is a tricky thing to understand, and it's something that needs to be prioritised with every piece of content you create.

Security

I didn't include this in the snippet previously, but Google's mission statement clearly states that they take the security of their users very seriously. This means everything from their data to their UX must be prioritised. It's easy to understand why this is. Would you trust someone who recommended a terrible restaurant? Or someone who gave you bad advice or put you in touch with a thief?

The same principle works here. It's bad business for Google if their search recommendations are leading people down unsafe paths. Your content container (a website, video page, etc.) needs to be up to date with regards to users' security needs.

Mobile Friendliness

When was the last time you searched for anything on a laptop? Now think back to how often you searched for something on your phone. Searching for something on the phone has become a reflex for us these days. The majority of Google's search volume now comes from mobile devices. A page that is not optimised for viewing on such a device is irrelevant since the user cannot access information easily.

This is why Google offers the choice of a 'simplified view' for websites that aren't mobile friendly. However, this is something that might soon disappear as you'll learn later in this book.

Structured Data

You want to be found on the internet, and Google wants to help you. This isn't because they're benevolent creatures. It's because the more relevant their search results are, the more their users will like them, and the more money they can make. Relevance is simply good business. In order to get found, you therefore need to help Google understand what your content is all about.

Google does a great job of figuring out what content is all about, but there are many things you can do to help it along the way. Structuring your data on your page (or content container) is a great way to do this. Ironically, most SEO advice centres around data structuring. If you've read anything about SEO, you'll have read about how keywords need to be placed in H1 tags, how the first paragraph matters, and so on.

This is important, but it misses the larger point about relevance. It's important for you to assimilate structured data into the bigger picture. You'll learn how to do this in the relevant chapter in this book.

Voice Search Optimised

This is a relatively new factor that is increasing daily. How often have you asked Google to retrieve results for you? How many times have you said 'Ok Google . . .' and asked something of your phone, be it traffic updates, weather updates, or some random piece of trivia you were arguing about with your friends?

Voice is the next area of development, and for once, Google is on the backfoot. Amazon's Alexa devices dominate the market, and Google is playing catch-up. The best way to reduce the gap is to present relevant data to their users, and as voice search demand grows, your content needs to be up to speed with it.

As I mentioned earlier, there are over two hundred factors that Google takes into account. A detailed discussion of this can be found on Brian Dean's blog at this link: https://backlinko.com/google-ranking-factors. I'm presenting this for the sake of completeness.

In order to succeed, you don't need to master all two hundred factors. Instead, focus on the factors I've presented just now. You'll learn more about all of them as you read this book, but remember that relevance is what is most important. That's the objective behind all SEO marketing. Don't get caught up in the technicalities of SEO.

Instead, focus on creating relevant content. Before creating anything, ask yourself what is it that your user wants to learn or view the most? Give them that and you'll take care of everything else automatically. This is a far easier way to reach the top of search results, as opposed to trying to game the system.

The factors that you'll read about in the rest of this book will help you design more relevant content and will help you enter the shoes of your user. You're going to learn specific steps that you can put into action to do this. The result will not only be a better understanding of SEO but more relevant content.

Chapter 2: Factor #1 – Search Intent

I've outlined briefly what search intent is in the previous chapter. In this chapter, I'm going to take you on a deeper tour of what it is and how you can tailor your content strategy to adhere to Google's requirements. Search intent is not always straightforward to decipher.

Type any search phrase into Google, and you'll see a number of results pop up. For example, let's say you search for 'best gaming laptop' on Google. The intent behind this search phrase is pretty clear. You want a list of the best laptops that are suited for gaming.

To this end, Google addresses your needs very well. Right on top, you receive a snippet that contains a list of the best gaming laptops. The rest of the page is filled with similar results. All of them contain lists of the latest and best gaming laptops. There are questions related to your search in the middle of the page. These questions are quite instructive when it comes to deciphering how Google looks at search intent.

The third question that Google lists is 'Are gaming laptops worth it in 2020?' This is not a question that is related to the search phrase, but it is a related search term. Remember that Google has tons of data, and clearly, they've noticed a trend. This is why they've presented this question as a possibly relevant search phrase. Perhaps people are moving away from buying gaming laptops to more social forms of gaming or are preferring VR gaming platforms.

The key is that these questions often help you develop more body to your content and give you points that you can address when creating content. For example, in this case you could develop a list of the best laptops. However, if you address the question of whether gaming laptops are worth it, Google will take notice of this and will boost your content. This is because it is more relevant than the other search results that don't address it.

Another way to determine search intent is to look at the list of related searches that Google gives you. At the bottom of our example search, you'll see suggestions such as 'best gaming laptops under $1,000' and so on. There is even a link to Reddit where gaming laptops are reviewed. Google clearly figures that providing a price limit suggestion as well as a trusted independent user review source adds relevance to the search query.

All of this is extremely valuable data for you to gather when conducting keyword research. This is something that has been written about extensively, so let's take a look at the best way to go about doing keyword research.

Keyword Research

The best way to optimise your content for search intent is to carry out intelligent keyword research. By intelligent, I mean that your process needs to be repeatable and reliable. This will save you a lot of time since keyword research can take you down rabbit holes that have no end. You want to spend as much time possible creating content, instead of trying to figure out what to create.

There are a number of tools that you can use to simplify keyword research. A few of these are:

1. Ubersuggest
2. Ahrefs
3. SEMRush
4. Long Tail Pro

All of these tools work well, but my preferred choice is Ubersuggest thanks to the number of free features available. The objective of keyword research is to find the best keywords to create content around. If you happen to be knowledgeable on a topic, you can go ahead and create content right away.

However, this isn't a very efficient way of doing things. If your aim is to run a business, you need to give your customers what they want. It's a bit like opening a restaurant and serving Greek food when your customers want French food. You can insist that Greek food is the best, but if your customers don't want to eat it, it doesn't matter how great a cook you are.

Keyword research also gives you insight into how quickly you can start ranking for topics. If a particular topic is extremely crowded and has been covered by major publications or competitors already, there's no point creating content there unless you can produce something that completely topples it.

For example, you can design the best sports car and paint it red, but people will still buy a Ferrari when given the choice. The only time they'll choose your car is if it completely blows a Ferrari out of the water. This is a tough task to do, even if it is achievable. It's far easier to create content around topics in your niche that have low competition but high search volume.

This is the stuff that users are searching for, but your competition hasn't got around to addressing yet. By creating a little niche for yourself in these topics, you'll build authority, after which you can expand into the more traditional areas of your niche. Everyone needs to grab a foothold somewhere, and these topics will be yours.

How to Conduct Keyword Research

I'm going to use Ubersuggest to demonstrate how you can conduct intelligent keyword research. You can replicate this process with pretty much every other search tool since the logic behind keyword research is the same. First, you want to enter search phrases related to what you want to create content around into Ubersuggest's search box. This tool will also give you the monthly search volume for these phrases.

Figure 1 below illustrates the search suggestions as well as volumes for the phrase 'best gaming laptop'. You can see that the tool provides 406 other suggestions for keywords along with the search volumes. You can also filter by language and location. The column named 'VOL' indicates search volume.

The columns after this are labeled CPC, PD, and SD. CPC stands for 'cost per click'. This is the estimated cost you'll have to pay if you used this search phrase to run an ad on Google. The CPC is a good indicator of how valuable a phrase is to advertisers. The higher the CPC is, the more advertisers are willing to spend on it. This indicates there's a valuable product that they're selling. After all, if they're willing to spend a lot on advertising, the profit margins must be high.

Next, we have PD. This stands for 'paid difficulty'. This is a measure of how competitive the paid search area is for this keyword. The higher the number, the more difficult it is. In our case, you can see it has a maximum level of 100. This means advertisers and sellers of gaming laptops are well aware of how lucrative this keyword is.

The next column is SD. This stands for 'SEO difficulty'. This is a measure of how tough it is to rank in Google's search listings. It takes the existing competition into account. This is the most useful metric for you in terms of SEO strategy. Notice that 'best gaming laptop' has a difficulty of 58, but 'best gaming laptop 2019' has a far lower difficulty of 39.

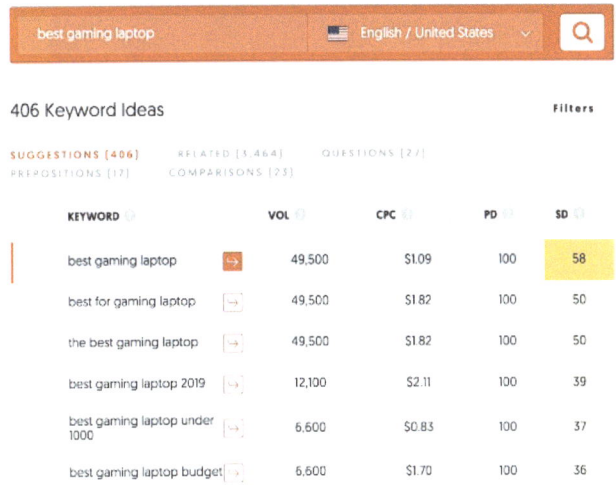

Figure 1: Ubersuggest Results for Best Gaming Laptop (Tchelet, 2020)

There is usually a correlation between the monthly search volume and the SD score. The higher the search volume is, the higher the domain authority of the pages creating content around them and the more difficult it is to rank for those phrases. However, this doesn't mean you can't write about the topic. Every once in a while, you'll find a very high search volume phrase with low competition.

It's far better to instead target medium search volume keywords that have low competition. All of the keyword phrases in Figure 1 that have a difficulty score under 40 are a good example of this. Obviously, you want to maximise the number of monthly searches and minimise the SD score.

Whichever keyword you select to create content around, it helps to take note of the other keywords. You want to include these keywords in your content so as to make it more relevant. Google takes this into account when evaluating your content for relevance. Think of your keyword and the related keywords as forming a keyword cloud that Google evaluates. The more relevant keywords there are in your cloud, the higher your article will rank on Google.

Competition

Another great way to find relevant keywords is to type the domain name of your competitors to see which keywords they rank for. Figure 2 illustrates how Ubersuggest helps you with this.

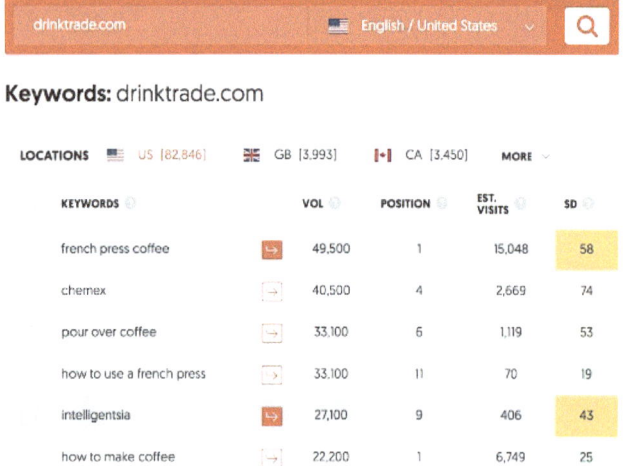

Figure 2: Keyword Results for drinktrade.com (Tchelet, 2020)

Use some of these keywords in your content to rank higher. For example, notice that 'how to use a French press' is a very specific keyword with an easily deciphered search intent. It has high search volume but a very low SD of 19. This is a great keyword suggestion for you to use.

Once you've gathered a good number of keywords using these methods, you want to sprinkle them throughout your content. You need to use these phrases in as natural a manner as possible. In the past, people could get away with stuffing keywords into their titles and text.

These days, this is a surefire way to make sure you get penalised by Google. For example, stuffing 'how to use a French press intelligentsia chemex' into a title leads to a terrible experience for the user. The title means nothing in plain English, after all. You want to sprinkle your keywords into the following places as naturally as possible:

- In the page title
- Within the first 100 words
- In a subheading
- Naturally sprinkled throughout the body

Chapter 3: SEO Factor #2 – Backlinks

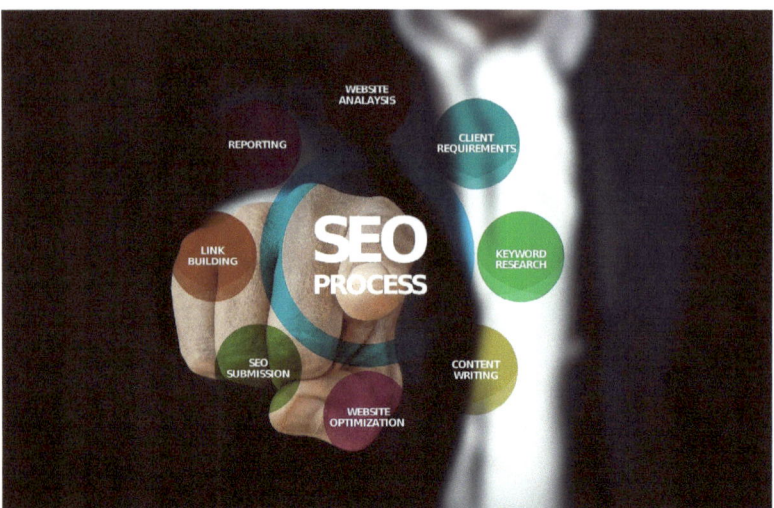

Backlinks are the web's way of providing your content with a vote of confidence. Backlinks are an essential part of Google's algorithm since they are not experts in every subject. What I mean is that if you ask Google what the best gaming laptop is, it's unlikely that Google as a company knows the answer. They don't know it any more than the person who wrote a dictionary does.

Their job is to evaluate the best sources of information, and backlinks are one way of determining which content seems relevant. If they notice that a website that contains the keywords 'best gaming laptop' has a number of backlinks to it, this website has more authority in their eyes.

A backlink is simply a link that one website places on its own page that leads to another. For example, if you place a link to ESPN on your website, you've provided them with a backlink. Remember the analogy about word-of-mouth marketing? That's really all a backlink is. It's someone expressing confidence in your content and thinking it has value.

Google sees this and promotes your content. The authority of the site that provides you with a backlink is a huge factor in Google's decision to promote you. Going back to word-of-mouth marketing, if a famous chef recommends you go to a particular restaurant, you're going to hold their opinion in higher regard than your neighbour Bob who doesn't know how to boil an egg.

If you happen to be writing something in the sports niche and ESPN links to your website, this is a huge plus in Google's eyes. ESPN is pretty close to the top in terms of authority, if not right at the top, and their vote of confidence means a lot. It solves the issue of Google having to take a guess on how good your content is.

A good link-building strategy is just as important as planning your keyword research. Remember that the most important thing of all is to create great content. All of the factors in this book are secondary to that. If you don't have great content that people will find helpful and will enjoy consuming, you won't succeed.

Relevance

When chasing backlinks, you want to get them from relevant websites, with preferably as high an authority as possible. If you're writing about sports and get a link from a website that writes about fish tanks, this isn't much of a vote of confidence. It's like Bob recommending a restaurant.

You can create great content and then hope that people link back to you over time, but it helps to pursue an active link-building strategy. This will help you grow a lot faster. The starting point is great content. What makes content great? Here are a few relevant points that will help you get started:

- It covers a subject more thoroughly than other pieces.
- It's authoritative (facts, studies).
- It's easy to consume (easy to read, well-designed).
- It's up to date.

A good way to think about your content is to ask yourself whether another person would want to share what you've created. Is it filled with helpful and insightful information? Or is it simply a copy-and-pasted version of an existing piece of content? When creating content, it helps to go in-depth as much as possible.

Many businesses opt to create small content pieces and hope this gives them some authority. Unfortunately, this doesn't always work. It's logical that longer-form content will naturally be more in-depth. Instead of creating four small pieces of content, it's much better to group all of them together and create a single, great resource.

This is what Google loves. You might think that readers don't like long pieces of content. After all, no one likes to spend fifteen minutes reading something. However, this is not how most consumers behave. Typically, a person will return to the content over time and gather relevant information from it.

They might not refer to every single piece of your article, but as long as they extract value from it, your content will do well. This is why long-form articles succeed. The objective isn't to simply write a lot. It's to write a lot of helpful stuff. If a topic demands an in-depth long-form article, then create this.

If a topic's issues can be addressed in as little as one thousand words, then this is fine as well. The depth and breadth of your content is what matters the most, not the length by itself. Make your content as long and as in-depth as it needs to be. The objective is for it to be useful, not to have it rank high.

A good way to determine how in-depth you want to go is to take a look at existing content and then figure out how you can outdo those pieces. Are they missing some important points? Is there something you can improve on? Take a note of these and design your content around these points.

Promotion

Creating content is one thing. This will bring traffic to you if you're creating great stuff and if people are finding value in it. However, a good way to jumpstart your growth is to actively promote your content. I'm not talking about social media here. Instead, you need to reach out to existing authorities in your niche with the intent of securing a backlink.

Here are a few ways to do this.

Active Outreach

Research websites in the same niche as yours and get in touch with those creators. Use this Email Outreach Guide when getting in touch with them. You want to do this in as nonspammy a manner as possible. Your objective is to introduce them to your content and inquire whether they'd be willing to link back to you.

Don't ask them in those words exactly. Perhaps share your content with them and ask for feedback on whether they found it useful. Or send them a piece of content that complements what they've already created. Always seek to add value to what they do, and they'll reciprocate.

Guest Post

You can guest post on active publications that allow contributions from various niche contributors or on someone else's blog. Whichever choice you pick, make sure you follow their submission guidelines. The owners of these publications are extremely busy and will reject your post if it violates the tiniest of guidelines.

It might not be a big deal to you, but respect their time and give them zero reasons to reject you. Some places prefer fully written articles upfront, while others ask you to send them ideas first. Once again, make sure you're adding value at all times.

Podcasts

See if you can book yourself a spot on a podcast. There are podcasts covering almost every niche, so take a look and see if someone would be willing to interview you. You don't need to be a celebrity to appear on these shows. In return, they'll leave you with a backlink to your website in their show notes.

Broken-Link Building

Very often, large websites link out to a variety of sources, and over time these sources either become irrelevant or those websites cease to exist. This leads to a broken link on the main website. You can use a tool such as Ahrefs to spot broken links, and then contact the owner of the main website asking them to link to you instead.

Your content should be relevant to what they were originally linking to, needless to say. This is a great way to build a high-quality backlink since they're already looking to replace a broken link, as opposed to providing you with a new one. Check out this Broken Link Building Guide for more details.

Resource Pages

Many large publications have resource pages that list a number of websites with helpful content. Check whether your website can be added to those pages. Make sure your content is relevant and adds value.

There are many ways of building links, but all of them come down to the same thing: building value. Focus on this, and you'll manage to generate high-quality backlinks in no time.

Chapter 4: SEO Factor #3 – Page Speed

As I mentioned earlier, the only thing worse than no internet is slow internet. Google takes page-loading speeds very seriously and actively monitors websites in this regard. A page that loads slowly is not considered relevant since it never gives users the chance to view its content. Therefore, it might as well not exist (as far as the user is concerned.)

The good news is that sorting out your page's loading speed is straightforward. This is the only portion of SEO that is straightforward and has clearly defined technical aspects to it. Fixing page speed is as simple as making sure a few technical details are in order and you're good to go.

The first step to take is to check your page's current performance. You can do this by using the free tool that Google provides at Test My Site. This tool will analyse your website's current performance statistics and will highlight any areas that it's lacking in. Another method of checking your website's performance is to connect it to Google's Search Console.

This has now been included under the wider umbrella of Google Webmasters. Simply search for these terms, and you'll be prompted to sign up for it. This tool helps you track not only the performance but also the indexing status of your site's content. Indexing refers to when Google officially recognises your content for the first time. It doesn't mean you'll rank high in search, but it indicates that Google knows you exist.

It's a great way to stay on top of your SEO since this tool gives you the search engine ranking of each article you create. Initially, all rankings will be high (a higher number indicates a lower result. A single digit equates to a position on the first page), but as time goes on and as backlinks to your content increase, you'll find yourself sliding up the rankings.

Once you've conducted the initial tests, it's time to perform some technical maintenance. If you're uncomfortable with doing these things, ask your webmaster to carry them out. If you don't use a webmaster, you can hire a developer and have them do these things for you.

Compress Images

Images are great things. They help your content have visual impact and can deliver information concisely. The fact is that most people process information a lot better when they're shown something as opposed to when they're asked to read it. Reading tends to result in deeper learning over time, but the average web user is not interested in the long term.

They want information right now and quickly. Images tick these boxes very well. The problem from a content creator's perspective is that they tend to be bulky, and this slows down the page-loading speed. A simple solution to this problem is to compress your images.

An image compressor will reduce the size of your images without sacrificing their quality. You can run pretty much any image file through this software including infographic files, which tend to be graphic heavy. If you're using WordPress to run your website, then you can use a plugin such as the WP Smush Image plugin to achieve this objective.

All you need to do is to install the plugin on your dashboard and activate it. The plugin automatically compresses your images without you having to manually feed them through it. Any future uploads can be processed through the plugin, and it will automatically compress them.

If you're using a platform other than WordPress, then check their app store to see if an image-compressing app is available. If it isn't, you can use tools such as TinyPNG or TinyJPG, which will do the same thing as the WordPress plugin. These tools won't integrate into your website automatically, but you can run your images through them and compress them before uploading them to your website.

Browser Caching

Caching occurs when tiny bits of your website are stored onto the visitor's computer. This way, when they revisit your website, these stored elements don't need to be reloaded. This drastically cuts down on page-loading times. You can implement browser caching by installing a WordPress plugin such as

W3 Total Cache . If you're using something other than WordPress, check with the platform's customer service to figure out how you can enable this feature.

Minify HTML

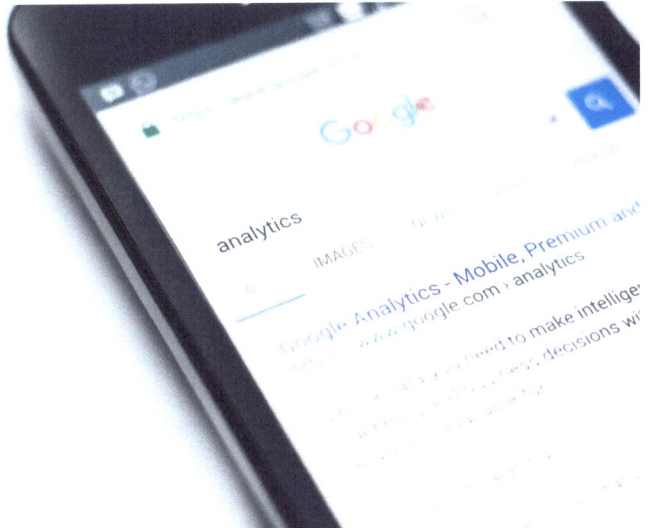

Much like how the design elements of your website need to be loaded when a person visits your website, the background HTML needs to be loaded as well. Having to load the HTML repeatedly when a person visits is a painful process that slows down page-loading speed immensely.

Just as you can cache design elements, you can minify HTML to prevent certain parts of code being repeatedly loaded. This reduces page load speed drastically (making it faster). You can do this on WordPress by installing the Minify HTML WordPress plugin. Other platform users will need to check with the relevant platforms to inquire how this can be done.

Remove Excess Plugins and Scripts

Plugins are great. They help you simplify a lot of tasks and seamlessly integrate themselves into your website's code. The problem is that if you install too many of them, they'll end up slowing down your website. At some point, every WordPress user has to decide which plugins they need and which ones they don't.

As tempting as it will be to hold on to every single one of them, you will need to sacrifice a few of them for the sake of page-loading speed. Reduce the number of them and watch how your website flies.

Use a CDN

CDN stands for 'content delivery network', and it's the most technical thing in this list. You will probably need the help of a developer if you don't know what a CDN is. The premise is simple. There are elements of your website that are static and others that are dynamic. For example, your website's homepage might remain pretty much the same, but the blog portion will change as you keep publishing content.

If a user in Korea accesses your website, which is stored in a server in the United States, this increases the page load speed. Registering for a CDN service allows you to store your website's static elements in a place closer to Korea so that more resources can be devoted to loading the dynamic portions of your website, and this allows it to load faster.

Some of the most popular CDNs are:

- Cloudflare
- MaxCDN
- Cloudwatch

Signing up for a CDN is as simple as creating an account. Making sure it's working for you is another task entirely. You need to log into the hosting panel of your website and set it up there to make sure your website is pointing to the CDN. Use a developer's help to do this.

Using a CDN is an easy win in terms of ensuring faster page load speeds, but it's something that many website owners neglect due to its technical nature. Do this and you'll ensure your page speeds increase massively.

Chapter 5: SEO Factor #4 – User Experience

User experience, or UX, is a truly vast field, and examining every element of it requires its own book. The good news is that with a few simple tweaks you can improve your rankings massively. Interpreting UX is as tough as figuring out search intent. How does Google know someone is satisfied with your website?

To achieve this, it uses an algorithm called RankBrain. Like with the search algorithm, the exact nature and workings of this are unknown. However, we can use common sense to figure out how it works. The key lies in understanding user behaviour. Think back to how you behave when you visit a website that you like.

Do you click away from it immediately or do you dwell on it for a while? Let's say you quickly clicked away from it. If you found the information you were looking for, you probably wouldn't click on any other search result. This means the page you visited, even if it was for a brief time, was relevant.

This is an important thing to note because many website owners automatically think that the longer the time a visitor spends on their page, the more relevant their content is. This isn't strictly true. Sometimes, visitors are looking for quick information. If your content is long-winded and doesn't provide them with an answer quickly (because you've designed it to keep them on the page for a long time), they'll spend a while looking for it and click back to the search results and click another result.

This is a bad thing for your relevancy ranking. My point is that while the time a user spends on your page is important, don't optimise your page for this. Instead, give them information quickly and easily. If they choose to spend time on your page, that's great. Even if they don't, as long as they don't click on some other search result, you'll rise in the relevancy rankings since you clearly gave them what they were looking for.

There are two metrics that are central to evaluating UX. Before looking at these, understand that there is a qualitative aspect to it. Is your website well designed and is it easy to read the content you've posted? Have you, for instance, posted white text with a blue background? Or a pink background? It's easy to go overboard with design elements that you think are quirky, but if it provides the user with a poor experience, it isn't worth it.

How often have you visited websites and had them bombard you with incessant pop-ups? You probably navigated away from the page quickly. What about pages that were inundated with ads and obstructed half the page with banners that advertised some product? Or what about websites that had videos that loaded automatically and started playing while you were reading their content?

All of these are examples of UX elements that are no longer acceptable. Google views such behaviour as a website prioritising monetisation over UX, and this is a huge no-no. Imagine visiting a store and having the salesperson immediately push you to buy a product without giving you any information on its features. You'll likely walk out immediately.

That's pretty much what UX is. So, take some time to look at your website through the eyes of a visitor and see what kind of an experience you're providing. Is your information well organised? Can the user clearly figure out how to get in touch with you in case of a question? Can they navigate to related content easily?

Think of it as you guiding your users down a path instead of pushing them down that path. You want to prompt them to move a certain way. If they choose not to, that's fine. After all, it's their choice.

Metrics

The quantitative side of UX is measured by two metrics, namely, CTR and dwell time. Let's look at these in more detail.

CTR

CTR stands for 'click-through rate'. Let's say an ad is shown five hundred times and is clicked five times. The CTR for this ad (5/500) is 1 percent. Similarly, how often your content's headlines are shown in search results and how often people end up clicking on it determines your CTR.

A higher CTR indicates to Google that your content is relevant. Since users will only see selected information in the search listings, it's important to optimise all of them to maximise your CTRs. These elements are:

- Page titles and headlines – These are what users first see when they look at your result in the search rankings. Use tools such as CoSchedule's Headline Analyzer. This will help you determine how effective your headlines are and how you can make them better.

- Page descriptions – This is the text that appears below the headline in the search result. Include your primary keyword in it, and make it as compelling as possible. Aim to communicate to the user that your page has exactly what they're looking for.

- URLs – Make your URLs short and sweet. Use the format www.example.com/primary-keyword. This clearly lets the user know what to expect when they click your page, and there's zero confusion.

Dwell Time

As I mentioned earlier, it's easy to get caught up in maximising dwell time, so don't fall for this trap. However, take note of the fact that it is an important metric. Dwell time is a measure of how long someone stays on your site once they click the link to it in the search results page.

This is closely linked to the bounce rate, which is a metric you'll see mentioned quite often. A high dwell time results in a low bounce rate. You want people to stay on your site for as long as possible. If they leave quickly, you want them to have received the information they were looking for as I explained at the beginning of this chapter.

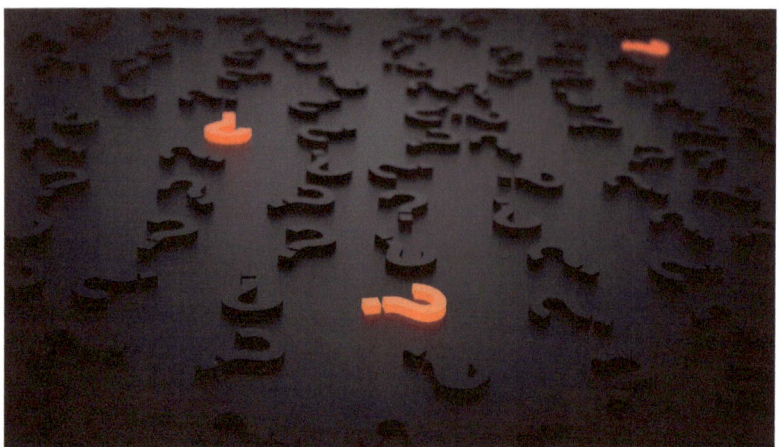

So how can you increase dwell time? It's pretty straightforward really. You create great content. Your content needs to have depth and breadth. This sounds tough to do, but examining your competition, especially the higher-ranking articles, will give you an idea of what to aim for. This will allow you to build upon that and create even better content.

Here are some ways you can improve the quality of your content.

Quick and Snappy Intros
Writing an introduction to a web article is not like writing one for a book. You want to get to the point as quickly as possible. The best intros pull readers into the problem even deeper by painting a picture that stands out vividly. They then quickly move on to describe what the article is going to help them with.

Long-Form Content
The longer your content is, the better your odds of addressing pressing issues. It's common sense, really. Your aim shouldn't be to write like Hemingway. Instead, your aim should be to convey as much information as possible. If a topic doesn't have enough meat on it to justify a long article, then you need to combine it with some other topic so that it brings more body to a larger topic.

This is why how-to guides and in-depth walkthrough content does so well. They hit all the pain points, and these articles are usually very well organised. The user is left in no doubt as to what they're getting. If they have specific questions, they can navigate directly to the relevant section and have their questions answered.

Easy to Read
Repeat after me: White space is good. You don't want to cram your page with large blocks of text.

It's perfectly fine to write two-sentence paragraphs like the one prior to this one.

Or like this.

Short, sharp sentences that stand out are what you should aim for.

Don't try to write long paragraphs, even if all the sentences relate to a similar topic. You might think grouping all of your ideas together will help organise information better, but this is not how people on the internet read. They skim lines to quickly figure out where the information they need is. They're not looking to spend fifteen to twenty minutes trying to figure out the point of your content. You can organise content using subheadings and so on. Never use blocks of text. This is a surefire way to turn people off and get them to click elsewhere.

Read this section again and ask yourself which portions were the easiest to read. The initial ones or the previous paragraph?

Videos and Alternate Content

Google wants you to help your users as much as possible. It rewards you if you place relevant YouTube videos or infographics that communicate related content to your readers. It shows you care about passing on information instead of trying to squeeze them for cash.

The great thing is that you don't need to embed your own videos in your article. Use someone else's video in there. This will boost their rankings, but it will boost yours as well since your intent is right.

Internal Links

Relevant and useful internal links to other content you've created are a great way to increase dwell time. Your readers will spend more time reading this content, and Google will view this as them receiving more value. It's also how you can strengthen your brand's perception with the reader.

Chapter 6: SEO Factor #5 – Content Quality

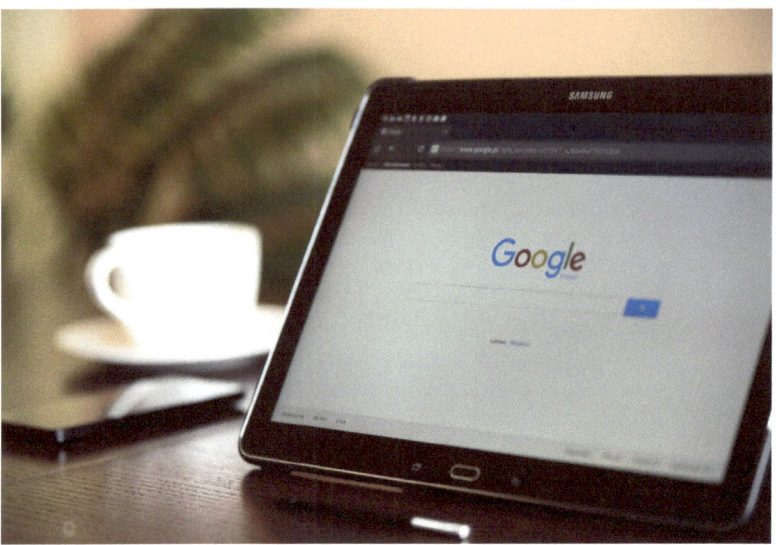

Like UX, content quality has many moving parts to it. There are a few ways to dissect how good your content is. This can be done by viewing it through three lenses: freshness, depth, and accuracy. Evaluate your content for these three things, and if you score favourably on all of them, your content is most likely going to be viewed by Google as being high quality.

Of course, you'll still need to make sure it's better than what's currently out there. The best way to ensure this is to either approach an issue from a different angle or bring your own unique spin on it. Make no mistake, Google will not reward run-of-the mill content. It aims to bring the best and highest quality content to its audience.

If you think you cannot create content of this caliber or if you think you don't have a unique take on a topic that can add value, it's best to move on and target something else. There's no point creating content that replicates what someone else is saying. Having gotten this out of the way, let's examine the three pillars of content quality.

Freshness

Google absolutely loves content that is regularly updated and maintained. This doesn't mean you need to release new versions of your article every day. It only applies to content that needs updating. For example, the SEO ranking niche is highly competitive because information changes regularly here.

A blog that was nowhere a year ago can reasonably rank in the top few spots if it manages to update its information before its competitors. In such cases, the freshness factor is high, and Google rewards them immediately. Another good example of this is in the sports niche, where people Google 'Latest NFL scores' or something of that kind.

Obviously, the intent here is to look at the latest scores, not scores from the previous season or highlights of last year's Super Bowl. Once you match search intent with freshness, Google will reward you handsomely. If you create any content that can be updated in the future, do so as soon as possible.

Accuracy

Content accuracy is something Google has been getting very good at verifying. In this age of fake news and conspiracy theories, it's something the company has been proactive about, unlike some of the other social media companies. For starters, Google classifies certain topics as being more factually sensitive than others.

Some of the common ones in this category are medical and financial topics. Google even refers to these topics as being YMYL (Your Money or Your Life) (Mccoy, 2016). If you're publishing content in these areas, you need to possess credibility. This means if you do not possess any qualifications to be talking about these topics, the chances of you ranking high are remote.

For example, if you're blogging about personal finance but are dispensing investment advice, your content will sink like a stone. However, if you clearly present information as being your own personal experience and as being a journey ('How I Got Out of Debt'), then Google has no issues with promoting your content.

With regards to health, it's even more sensitive. Qualifications need to be clearly displayed on the page, and all information is fact-checked against a repository called the Knowledge Graph. This is a huge repository of information from factually verified and credible sources that Google has collected information from over the years. If there is a disagreement between your facts and these verified facts, Google will suppress your results unless you manage to bring more authority to the subject.

Outside of YMYL, Google has strict guidelines for content accuracy. There are certain niches where it's impossible to verify accuracy (spirituality, etc.), but your content needs to be helpful and shouldn't promote inaccurate information. All it takes is one user to report your site for spreading nonsense, and if Google finds upon investigation that this is true, you'll likely suffer.

The thing for you to do is ensure you link to verified and trusted sources in your niche. Use in-text links so that Google can clearly see who you're linking out to. If your topic is YMYL, then it's a good idea to list a separate reference section as a footnote (in addition to in-text links) to make it very clear that you're checking your content for accuracy.

Depth

Your content needs to go deep into a subject while also being broad. Some content creators get confused about how this works and end up creating confusing content. Here's how you can structure your content strategy. First, aim to address a wide breadth of topics in your niche through different pieces of content.

Next, dive deep with every piece of content. For example, let's say you're running a website about mattresses and are examining issues surrounding sleep quality and conditions that affect sleep. In terms of breadth, you would have to cover medical issues such as sleep apnea and insomnia, lifestyle issues such as alcoholism and poor sleep conditions, and also devices that can help people get a better night's sleep.

This gives you the breadth you need. Now, when you create an article about sleep apnea, make sure you dive deep into the topic. You might think that researching the history of how sleep apnea was first diagnosed is a waste of time, but it fulfills the need for depth. Not all of your readers might want to read it, but include it anyway.

The only exception is if this information is not relevant in any way. If you can draw lessons from the history of sleep apnea diagnosis and use it to paint a fuller picture of how the condition is diagnosed these days, this is very helpful information. If you're going to simply list a bunch of dates and names, then this isn't relevant. Aim to paint a picture at all times.

Explore every aspect of it and provide all kinds of helpful information. You could link to a YouTube video about the subject and also include pictures and an infographic about what it is. Make it shareable so that your readers can spread it on their social media accounts.

Look at the topics on sleep apnea currently out there, and examine the questions that Google provides. Look at the suggestions at the bottom of the first page to get a better idea of how you can structure your content. All of this will give you a well-rounded and deep article.

Before creating this content, take some time to develop an outline. Weave a narrative before you begin writing. Remember, you don't need to write as if you're competing against a Booker Prize finalist. Instead, aim to convey information in as helpful a manner as possible. Structure enough white space between your paragraphs so that your readers can consume information easily.

List all of your sources and link to them. If there's something that is unclear to you, admit it. This is a very underrated way of gathering feedback from your audience. Oftentimes, you'll see comments under blog posts clarifying information in it, and it's a good way to build a relationship with your audience.

I'm not saying you should do this deliberately. The point is to be genuine. Do all of this, and depth will take care of itself. Sometimes, you'll have a take on a topic that isn't covered by Google's suggestions, or you might even find that Google is suggesting something that is not related to the topic or is presenting it in the wrong way.

Don't be afraid of taking a negative stance in this regard. As long as you can back up your information and you can present sources properly, you have nothing to worry about. Make sure your information is as accurate as possible at all times.

Your SEO rankings will take care of themselves automatically. Many content creators do this the other way around. They start by looking at how they can rank high and try to reverse engineer the process technically. They stuff keywords and other keyword suggestions into their posts, and the end result is something that is low quality.

If a user navigates to your page, clicks away from it, and clicks something else, Google immediately knows your content is not up to scratch. They don't need to read the words on your page to be able to know this. Evaluate your content along these lines, and you'll end up creating great stuff all the time.

Chapter 7: SEO Factor #6 – Site Authority

Site authority is something that takes time to build, but it doesn't take as long as some beginners think. The best way to understand site authority is to return to our previous example of restaurant recommendations. A famous chef who knows what they're talking about is more likely to provide better recommendations than someone who doesn't know how to boil an egg.

Google treats all information in the same manner. If anything, the company gives a huge weight to site authority because there's no way it can know anything about the information that is being searched. Google's algorithm isn't designed to learn the vast amounts of information that is present on the internet.

It isn't trying to become an encyclopedia. Its role is more that of an efficient librarian. If you have a question, the librarian's role is to direct you as quickly as possible to the relevant source. In order to do this, she needs to consistently direct people to the highest sources of authority.

Many website owners get authority all wrong because their focus is far too broad. In some cases, they get their niches wrong as well and don't take the necessity of authority seriously enough. Let's take a deeper look at some of these niches.

YMYL

You've already learned that YMYL stands for Your Money or Your Life. Google's YMYL categories go beyond just medical and financial issues, though. Even issues such as politics or anything even tangentially related to health, such as sleep quality, are treated with extreme care.

If you happen to have a website in these niches, you need to consider your own authority. You need to possess a professional qualification from a recognised body in order to provide advice. In the case of personal finance, Google recognises that people can document their personal journeys, and as long as they aren't providing professional services with regards to debt management and so on, it doesn't have issues promoting such content.

The same applies to fitness-related content. If you're designing workout programs for people and selling them, you need to have credentials. However, if you're documenting your fat-loss journey (for example) and are simply recommending other services, this is fine.

Nutrition falls under this category as well. You can provide recipes and sell your cookbooks; however, Google will take issue if you promote your recipes for weight-loss diets without backing it up with relevant credentials. The best way to provide credentials is to link your social media profiles prominently on your website.

If you have a LinkedIn profile that clearly states your credentials or if you can provide a short bio with a link that displays your credentials, this is a good way to let Google know of your authority. Keep in mind that doing this only gets your foot in the door. It's not as if you'll vault up to the first place because of this.

Your content's quality still matters. It's just that YMYL topics require you to have credentials to get started. If you don't have credentials, then you need to tailor your content in such a way that it's very clear to a reader that you're not a professional and that you're merely presenting your own experiences.

A standard disclaimer does the trick. Make sure you have it prominently displayed everywhere so that you don't run into issues down the road. You will see some personal finance websites without this disclaimer, but these will invariably be older websites that have enough user loyalty built up that they're not dependent on organic search traffic anymore.

Keys to Authority

No matter what your niche is, you need to demonstrate authority. So how do you do this? Saying that your content needs to be authoritative is easy enough. Demonstrating authority is another thing entirely. To better understand this, we need to step back and look at how authority is interpreted in the physical world.

If someone tells you to display your ID, will you do it automatically? Or will you ask them for an appropriate credential? Next, if someone voices their opinion about something, what are the factors you'll take into consideration before accepting their points? You'll probably look at whether other people agree with them and the quality of those people.

If they're a prominent personality, you'll take this into consideration as well. Lastly, you'll make sure that what they're saying actually makes sense. The same principles apply in Google's algorithm.

Backlinks tick a lot of these boxes. For starters, they indicate people think you know what you're talking about. They show that people are willing to refer others to you. The people linking to you are providing you with word-of-mouth recommendations, and this is why Google values them so highly. In order to be an authority, or sound authoritative, you need to have backlinks.

Next, your content needs to be top notch. This is something that is obvious. As long as your content is great and provides value according to the guidelines I've already provided, you'll manage to attract a steady stream of users to your website. This is where many website owners stumble, though.

They create great content and they receive decent traffic, but Google doesn't consider them as being very authoritative. Why is this? It has everything to do with the focus of their content. Let's say you're writing about the best travel destinations for next summer for couples looking to splurge a little cash on luxury vacations, posh destinations, and so on.

You compile a great list of places chock-full of helpful information, tips on how to get there, off-beat activities, and so on. However, you still don't rank for that search term even after a year. What's going on here is that Google looks at your content and realises that it's in the same niche as Jetsetter and other Condé Nast publications.

If you're a user searching for great luxury travel tips, are you more likely to visit Jetsetter's website or a random travel blog that isn't anywhere near as popular? No matter how great your content is, the user is still going to trust a much larger publication. The point is, you should seek to narrow and niche your content down. Here's what Google says in their SEO Starter Kit (*Search Engine Optimization (SEO) Starter Guide*, 2020, Act in a way that cultivates user trust Section, para. 2):

> A site with a good reputation is trustworthy. Cultivate a reputation for expertise and trustworthiness in a specific area . . . Expertise and authoritativeness of a site increases its quality. Be sure that content on your site is created or edited by people with expertise in the topic. For example, providing expert or experienced sources can help users understand articles' expertise. Representing well-established consensus in pages on scientific topics is a good practice if such consensus exists.

There's no point in going after broad audiences unless you have the money to buy traffic and establish massive authority by hiring publicists to vouch for you. Instead of writing about luxury destinations around the world, focus on one particular resort and go in-depth, as mentioned earlier.

You'll manage to establish a high level of authority here since no one else is likely writing about things to such a level. Any magazine can send one of their writers on a trip to a few resorts. How many take the time to profile a single location or a hotel and go deep into it? Unless the place happens to be historically significant, this never happens.

Similarly, if you're writing about something in the technology niche, don't go too broad. There's no way you can compete with Techcrunch or Wired. Instead, focus on a narrow niche and become the biggest authority in that sector. You might not know everything about the best gaming laptops around.

However, you do know what is the best graphics card that allows gamers to extract the highest level of performance from their games. Not only that, you also know how each and every graphics card on the market compares against one another, and you've reviewed each of them. This is a particularly narrow topic, but you get the idea.

Don't mistake my previous advice of going broad to mean that you need to cover your entire niche. Cover your niche by all means, but make sure your niche itself is focused and has a strong core audience. For example, instead of covering college football, cover the performance of the Ohio State Buckeyes' defense and their respective coaches.

The degree to which you'll niche down depends on the broader niche. Sports for example is a very broad niche, and there is a lot of competition in it. For instance, football has a lot of publications. However, dirt biking isn't as competitive. You could reasonably cover this space along with tips that are niche appropriate.

So, take the time to determine your focus. This will help you establish authority a lot faster in Google's eyes, and you'll be able to provide better content since you won't be trying to do everything at once.

Chapter 8: SEO Factor #7 – Security and Mobile Friendliness

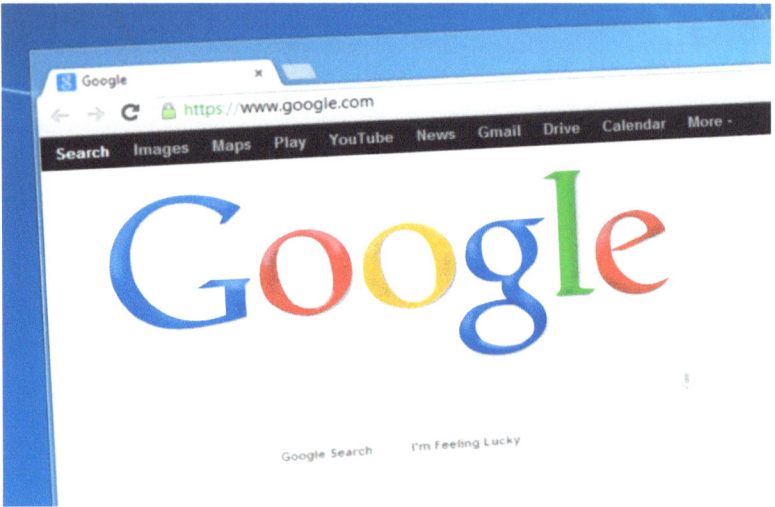

Security and mobile friendliness are extremely important components when it comes to your ability to rank well in search. These are typically implemented by your website provider, but if they aren't, this chapter is for you.

Security

As I previously highlighted, Google takes the security of its users seriously. This is common sense, really. They don't want to send people to a website that is spammy and is likely to infect their computers with viruses or collect data and use it without proper consent. If you've ever used Chrome, you've probably received the 'Not Secure' warning when attempting to access such websites.

It's telling that Google makes it hard for you to bypass this page. There is no immediate option Chrome provides you with to skip past this page and continue to a website anyway. This page is typically shown on websites that haven't encrypted the data between the browser and the server.

The simplest way to figure out whether a site is encrypted is to look at the address bar. If you see an 'https' in the address, it's secure. Chrome also displays a small padlock prior to the address to indicate a secure website. As a website owner, making sure your site is secure is quite easy.

You need to install an SSL certificate. This will turn your address into the 'https' format. Your hosting provider can do this for you free of charge. Alternatively, you can use Let's Encrypt, which is a free SSL certificate provider that you can install. Even if you can't do this yourself, your webmaster will be able to.

Installing an SSL is the first step. The next thing to do is to make sure you're complying with all privacy-related laws. This means your Privacy Policy should be up to date and must list everything you do with your visitors' data. Termsfeed is a service that allows you to generate a fully compliant privacy policy. If you're using any advanced analytics trackers, you'll need to pay to generate one on their website. However, the investment is worth it since you can be held legally liable for any privacy violations.

Your privacy policy should be contained in a page that is easily accessible and where users can quickly find it. Most website owners choose the link to their policies on their footers. This is an acceptable location according to Google's guidelines.

You can also link to your Terms and Conditions page from there as well. You don't need to have this necessarily, and it depends on what your business is. Make sure you're fully compliant with regards to the latest versions of privacy laws, such as the General Data Protection Regulations (GDPR) that have been enacted in the European Union. America doesn't have any similar laws as yet, but it's only a matter of time.

The best way to ensure full GDPR compliance is to install plugins that help you with this. At the very least, you should be gathering your visitors' consents to store cookies and should offer them a choice to allow this or not. Software providers such as WordPress, Wix, and Squarespace already have fully GDPR-compliant platforms, but it's up to you to make sure your customer-facing website has the appropriate notices and storage policies.

Whether you recognise it or not, Google already treats customer data in the same manner as a bank treats your money. Show that you take it just as seriously as they do and you won't have any privacy or security-related issues. If you accept payments on your website, your payment gateway providers need to be compliant as well. Make sure you sign up with trusted providers who you know can be relied on in this regard.

Mobile Friendliness

Mobile is utterly dominant when it comes to search. Most people use their phones to search for information, and it is important for your website to be mobile friendly. Most website owners optimise their mobile performance and treat the desktop performance as being secondary.

I don't recommend going to this extreme, but your website's mobile performance is far more important than the desktop version's. The only exception is if your website and business is in a B2B (business to business) niche. For everything else, focus on mobile UX development and performance.

An easy way to evaluate mobile performance is to look at what Google tells you in the Search Console. Here, you can view data on mobile page responsiveness and performance.

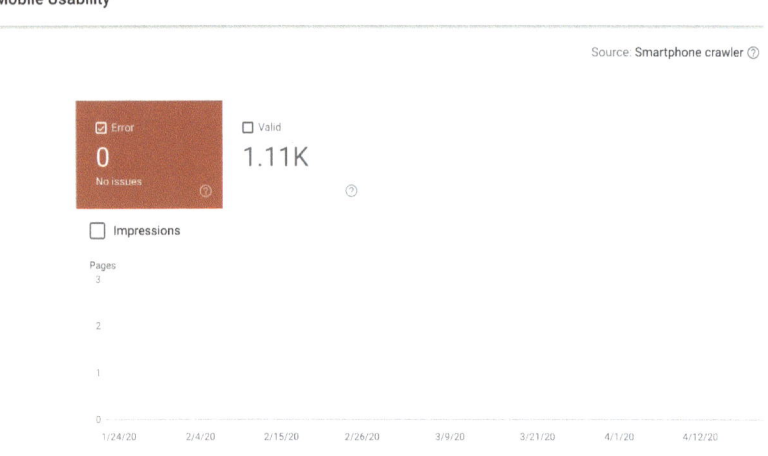

Figure 3: Google Search Console's Mobile Performance Report.

Optimising for mobile sounds like it's something complicated, but it's as simple as making sure your users have a good experience in terms of navigation and design. Make sure your information is neatly organised and that the text is easy to read. If you're selling a product, how well are its features highlighted?

Is your return policy and shipping policy well highlighted? These things matter a lot to consumers, so take the time to make sure your website is designed well. If you're using WordPress or any other website builder, take the time to adjust the mobile designs. While these platforms do a good job of ensuring the designs carry over, not all elements translate well. In some cases, you might have to redesign certain elements to make sure they're more mobile friendly.

Always check the Search Console to make sure your pages are loading quickly and are performing well. Often, fancy design elements can hamper performance. It's better to have a fast-loading website that is decent looking than a slow website that is stunning. I'm not saying you can get away with an ugly website, but functionality is far more important than some cool colours. Take a look at how the major tech companies present themselves on their website, and you'll understand how important functionality and utility is to their users. For example, all of Google's pages have tons of whitespace, and the information is presented clearly. Copy this formula and you'll see your website soar in the rankings.

Chapter 9: SEO Factor #8 – Structured Data

Text on a page is easy for humans to read but tough for machines to parse. Google has long suffered from this problem, and no matter how smart their algorithm gets, it's probably not going to equal human reading capabilities anytime soon. In earlier times, website owners would game the algorithm by stuffing keywords in all the obvious places.

For example, if someone searched for 'best dog food', Google would be liable to return a result that contained this exact expression pasted in a nonsensical manner. It made sense to the algorithm but hardly made sense from a human relevance perspective. To bridge this gap, Google has provided website owners with a structured data template.

It doesn't fit every single niche as yet, but there are many, such as cooking and recipes, that it fits very well with. If you were to search for a recipe right now, Google will be able to show you a sample recipe in a snippet along with the cooking time and the calories.

This is because the owner of that page has structured their data in such a way so as to help Google retrieve this information easily. Some of the other niches structured data helps are:

- Books
- Movies
- Courses
- Ratings
- Events
- Local business info
- And much more

Understanding Structured Data

To help provide webmasters with better tools to have their content highlighted, Google offers a free tool called the <u>Structured Data Markup Helper</u>. Using this tool, you simply add the data that Google prompts you to add, in the format it demands, and you're all good to go. You can then copy-paste the code back into your website.

If you're technically challenged, it might be best to hire a developer to do this for you. Once your webpages are structured data friendly, they'll be more likely to show up as a snippet or a rich snippet result.

This is an area that Google has been experimenting with quite a lot. The ultimate aim is to make their results even more relevant. This is why you might have noticed that aside from text snippets, search results now contain all sorts of information that present a webpage in a more accurate way.

With regards to structured data, change is afoot. Using structured markup is one way of deriving data for a rich snippet, but Google has been experimenting with other methods. To this end, it recently moved a tool called the 'Rich Results Test' out of beta and into live mode.

The structured data tool is still supported and will be used for a few years, but it will be phased out at some point (Southern, 2020). According to Google, the Rich Results tool offers a number of advantages over the structured data tool.

For starters, it provides better feedback to website owners and fully integrates with the Search Console. This way you can test your webpage for its attributes much more easily. The other major improvement is that the tool optimises your page for both mobile and desktop equally well.

This points to Google giving importance to mobile search over desktop search. In addition to this, the rich text tool allows webmasters to test snippets of code, should they choose to, instead of an entire URL. The message from Google is loud and clear. Moving forward, it's best to start relying on the rich text tool.

For now, though, the structured data tool still rules. If you happen to be operating in one of the niches mentioned above, it's best for you to ask your developer to utilise this tool and to optimise your page for the best results. The benefits of your page being showcased in a rich snippet are massive.

Rich snippets are shown at the top of the page and are far more prominent than text-based results. You stand a much better chance of receiving huge amounts of traffic by showing up in one of these.

Chapter 10: SEO Factor #9 – Voice Search Optimization

When was Paul Newman born? What time is my favourite movie playing? Is iced water good for dogs? When and why did The Beatles break up? People are beginning to ask these questions directly to Google with greater frequency.

As I mentioned in the beginning, voice search is the next major area of development. With AI constantly making progress, it's a matter of time before we start to think of Google as a voice-driven engine rather than something we type words into. It isn't just Google. Companies such as Amazon and Microsoft have also developed their own voice search assistants that are driving user behaviour in their products.

Currently, Amazon's Alexa is dominant, but this is used mostly for shopping-related queries. Google still rules the roost when it comes to search queries, and the company has been making massive strides in boosting its algorithm.

As a website owner, it's in your best interests to make your content as friendly as possible for Google to read. If you've ever asked Google to search for something by asking it directly, you'll know that the assistant reads the answer back to you. This is a huge clue with regards to the direction your content needs to go in.

There are a few simple guidelines you can use to make your content more voice-search friendly. Remember that this is a growing area, so there will be developments that will occur at a rapid pace in the next few years.

Create FAQ Pages

Most questions are asked in a specific format. They're usually sentences that end with a question mark and request a specific answer. You can provide these answers in a frequently asked questions (FAQ) section. Consider including a section in all of your blog posts. Not only will this help summarise the content for your readers, it will also give Google an easy way to match the question to your FAQ content directly.

It also tells Google that the answer is right there for it to relay to the user. This makes the algorithm's job a lot easier, and Google will favour such results. There's no evidence as yet that this technique will help you score major improvements. However, this is probably because the field of voice search is still growing, and we're in nascent stages at this point.

You don't need to shoehorn FAQ sections everywhere. Just add them wherever they make sense. Keep user convenience at the top of your mind at all times, voice search or not.

Capture the Snippet

The featured snippet at the top of the page is what Google often uses to relay answers to voice search queries. If you want to have your content highlighted, it's best to shoot for the snippet. The question is how do you capture this spot?

The marketing firm HubSpot ran an experiment to determine this exactly. You can read about it at <u>this guide by HubSpot</u>. Here are some of the things that the company recommends.

Clean HTML

This goes back to my earlier point about your code needing to be as organised and efficient as possible. Snippet information is usually a direct answer to a particular question. It's a good idea to provide a brief answer to the primary question your post is trying to address. This way users get the information they need, and Google notices this and promotes your content further.

Formatted H2 and H3 Headers

This is especially the case with listicles. For example, an article about the best speeches ever made will prompt Google to gather a list of headings in an article and display them in the snippet. The idea is to motivate the user to click that snippet and read the entire article. If your list happens to be poorly formatted and isn't easy to read, the user is likely to scroll down and click something else.

The lesson here is for you to optimise your H2 and H3 headers and to make sure the titles are succinct and to the point. By cleaning these up, you'll increase your chances of showing up in the snippet.

Crafted Content

The biggest difference-maker is the way your content is structured and the depth to which it goes. When creating content around a topic, examine if from a when, where, why, what, who, and how perspective. According to HubSpot, this gives you a great shot at landing the snippet since a question is likely to be centred around these questions.

Take a look at the current search results. If there's a snippet, is it a paragraph or a list? This tells you what Google's looking for. If it's a list, you know that you need to clean your headers. If it's a paragraph, aim to provide the answer early in your article.

For example, if someone searches for optimal YouTube thumbnail sizes, give them the answer early in the article. However, there's clearly more to creating a YouTube thumbnail than simply sizing a photograph correctly. You can tell them this and dive into the different sizes that might work depending on the niche and content being created.

Many content creators think providing the answer upfront reduces dwell time and this is a bad thing. As explained previously, this is the wrong way to think about how Google works. The aim is to be helpful and provide value. Trying to increase dwell time by not providing the answer upfront is trying to game the system, and eventually Google will catch on to what you're doing.

Don't be one of those people who live in fear of Google's latest updates. Instead be as helpful as possible, and you'll have nothing to worry about.

Write Naturally

I mentioned previously that you don't need to write like Hemingway or some famous author to succeed at SEO. Your tone of voice should be as natural as possible. In fact, writing well (in the traditional sense) might actually hurt your chances of ranking well.

This is because a voice search query demands an equally casual and appropriate response. How would you react if you asked someone a question and they began with 'Four score and seven years ago . . .'? They might tell you what you want to know, but you're likely not going to approach them with a question again.

Google wants to avoid such an experience. If it has to read back an extremely formal and novel-like answer, that's not going to cut it. When writing content, think of it as you explaining something to your neighbour. They asked you a question, and you're just trying to help them out. That will help you get your tone right.

Keep it Simple

Some content creators fall into the trap of trying to impress everyone with the vocabulary. You're not a lawyer or a contract writer. You're a content creator. There's a huge difference. Your aim is to keep it simple, not complicate simple things needlessly. Use everyday language in all of your sentences.

The analogy of explaining things to your neighbour is powerful here because it helps you get the message across as if you're talking to a human being. The average reading level, and it hurts to write this, is at a ninth-grade level. Most people are not keen on reading heavy stuff. Unless the topic demands it, stick to basic words and keep it simple.

Boost Speed

When someone asks Google a question, it needs to scan the web for relevant results, and then needs to read back that answer. The response time is about the same as a text-based search, but there's an additional task in there that Google needs to do. It needs to read the answer back in a reasonable amount of time without making it awkward.

Imagine asking someone a question and them staring off into space for a minute. Again, even if they provide you with the right answer, you're not going to ask them a second time. This is why site speed is so important. It allows Google to quickly scan your content for the answer and relay that back to the user. If your content is helpful, Google looks smart and everyone's happy.

Conclusion

This brings to a close our look at the various factors that drive SEO success. You're probably raring to go and implement all of these things on your website. Before you do, I'd like to provide a few words of advice. SEO is a long-term game. It doesn't give you instant results like paid ads do.

SEO is all about enticing people to come visit you. Think of it this way. If I placed a chocolate cake in front of you, and if you happen to love chocolate cake, you'd be tempted to gobble it up. What if I placed it in front of you all the time? You'd keep eating it, and your health would deteriorate. You'd have to work very hard to stay fit under such circumstances.

However, what if you worked out a healthy eating plan? You wouldn't see results immediately, but over the long term, staying healthy will be a lot easier for you. You'll develop great habits, and you won't find it as tough as the person who eats chocolate cake all the time.

This is what paid ads versus SEO is like. Paid ads give you instant satisfaction, but if you're going to rely on them over the long term, you're going to have to work hard to sustain any sort of advantage. SEO gives you the luxury of sitting back and waiting for your customers to come to you. It costs nothing compared to paid ads.

The catch is you need to wait a while for it to start taking effect. Expecting overnight results is not the correct way to go about it. Keep creating high-quality content even if you hear crickets on your website. You'll feel as if you're writing to a ghost town, but trust the process. Over time, Google will begin to reward you, and you'll start to see people visiting your website.

As traffic picks up, engage them and create the content they love. This will build a virtuous circle, and soon, you'll have Google rewarding you with free traffic for a long time. Keep implementing all of the tools and techniques you've learned about in this book, and you'll surely hit the #1 spot on the search rankings list.

I wish you all the luck in the world with your SEO efforts!

References

Bernazzani, S. (2014). *The Decline of Organic Facebook Reach & How to Adjust to the Algorithm*. Hubspot.Com. https://blog.hubspot.com/marketing/facebook-organic-reach-declining

How Google Search Works | Our Mission. (2019). Google.Com. https://www.google.com/search/howsearchworks/mission/

Mccoy, J. (2016, January 4). *What Are EAT and YMYL: New Google Search Guidelines Acronyms*. SEMrush Blog. https://www.semrush.com/blog/eat-and-ymyl-new-google-search-guidelines-acronyms-of-quality-content/.

Southern, M. (2020, July 7). *Google Shutters Structured Data Testing Tool*. Search Engine Journal. https://www.searchenginejournal.com/google-rich-results-structured-data-test-tool/373903/#close

Google(n.d.). Relevance Definition. https://support.google.com/google-ads/answer/14089?hl=en

Image References

magnifying-glass-earth. (2020). In *pixabay*.

business-computer. (2020). In *pixabay*.

search-internet-online-web-browser. (2020). In *pixabay*.

electronics-mobile-phone-screen. (2020). In *pixabay*.

seo-search-engine-optimization. (2020). In *pixabay*.

google-www-online-search. (2020). In *pixabay*.

/logo-google. (2020). In *pixabay*.

needle-in-a-haystack. (2020). In *pixabay*.

o-google-search-engine. (2020). In *pixabay*.

online-marketing-internet-marketing. (2020). In *pixabay*.

question-mark. (2020). In *pixabay*.

search-engine-browser. (2020). In *pixabay*.

search-engine-tablet. (2020). In *pixabay*.

search-help-faq. (2020). In *pixabay*.

seo-google. (2020). In *pixabay*.

seo-google-search-engine-browser. (2020). In *pixabay*.

seo-optimization-. (2020). In *pixabay*.

seo-search-engine-optimization-. (2020). In *pixabay*.

seo-sem-marketing. (2020). In *pixabay*.

window-hand-magnifying-glass. (2020). In *pixabay*.

www.ingramcontent.com/pod-product-compliance
Lightning Source LLC
Chambersburg PA
CBHW040327220526
45473CB00009B/2599